STO

FRIENDS
OF ACPL

IAN SERRAILLIER

ROBIN AND HIS MERRY MEN

Ballads of Robin Hood

Illustrated by
VICTOR G. AMBRUS

NEW YORK
HENRY Z. WALCK, INC.

```
398.2   Serraillier, Ian
  S         Robin and his merry men; illus. by
        Victor G. Ambrus.    Walck, 1970
          64p.  illus.

          First pub. in England in 1969.  Com-
        panion vol. to; Robin in the greenwood.
          Retelling, in verse, of the ballads
        of Robin Hood.


        1. Robin Hood   I. Illus.   II. Title
```

To Andrew

CONTENTS

Guest of Honour

A Sackful of Silver

The Sheriff's Revenge

The King's Pardon

Guest of Honour

I THE SORROWFUL STRANGER

Come, gather round and listen awhile
   To a tale of the good greenwood
And a courteous yeoman, a brave outlaw,
   Whose name was Robin Hood.

One morning he was in Barnsley Dale
   Under his trysting tree,
Beside him valiant Little John,
   A bearded giant he;

Will Scarlet too, whose feathered cap
   Was a scarlet flame in the sun;
And, staunch and true as the greenwood oak,
   Much, the miller's son.

'Master,' said Little John, 'we have fish
  And venison, sparkling wine.
Sit down and eat.' Said Robin Hood,
  'I have no wish to dine,

'Till I've welcomed to my table here
  Some strange and unknown guest,
Some baron, squire, or wealthy knight
  With money to pay for the best.'

'Which way shall we go,' said Little John,
  'This unknown guest to find?
Whom shall we rob and strip of his gold?
  Whom shall we beat and bind?'

'O, use no force,' said Robin Hood,
  'But courtesy you must show;
And lay no hands on the labourer
  Who toils with wagon and plough,

'On farmer, peasant, or yeoman brave,
  And all who take delight
In field and hill and the good greenwood;
  Touch no squire or knight.

'But bishops and archbishops, I say,
  Them shall you beat and bind;
And the proud Sheriff of Nottingham,
  Him chiefly bear in mind.

'Take Scarlet and Much and, bow in hand,
  Walk to Watling Street,
And wait there under the trees until
  Some guest you chance to meet.

'Be he abbot or earl or mincing lord
  Or haughty baron,' he said,
'Bring him here to my trysting tree—
  I'll have a banquet spread.'

Straightway they walked to Watling Street,
  Those sturdy yeomen three;
They looked to the east, they looked to the west,
  But nobody could they see.

Then as they looked down Barnsley Dale
  Where the wood was dark and drear,
By bramble, briar and branch they saw
  A Knight come riding near.

Sad was his face and woe-begone,
  He knew no pomp or pride;
One foot stood in the stirrup, the other
  Dangled limp at his side.

His tattered hood hung over his eyes,
  Begrimed was his array;
He was the sorriest knight that ever
  Rode on a summer's day.

'Welcome, sir, to the good greenwood,'
  Said John on bended knee.
'Greetings from my master, Sir Knight,
  From my two friends and me.'

'Who is your master?' asked the Knight.
  John answered, 'Robin Hood.'
'Robin Hood? Of your master, sir,
  I have heard men speak much good.

'Although I had meant to dine today
  At Blyth or Doncaster,
My brothers, I'll gladly go with you,
  Your company proudly share.'

2 THE BANQUET

Deep was the wood where he turned his horse;
   Deeper still were his sighs,
As over his care-worn cheeks the tears
   Ran streaming down from his eyes.

At last they came to the greenwood oak,
   Where Robin on bended knee
Took off his hood and bowed his head,
   Greeting him courteously.

Together they washed and dried their hands,
  Together sat down to dine
On liver and lungs and heart of the deer,
  With flagons of ale and wine,

Turbot and lamprey, pheasant and swan
  Roasted over the fire,
And pigeon pie from the tastiest birds
  Ever perched on branch or briar.

'My thanks, good sir. I've not eaten so well,'
  Said the Knight, 'for three weeks past.
And when I return you shall be my guest—
  I promise you shall not fast.'

'You flatter me, sir,' said Robin Hood.
  'Yet think you my greed is such
I expect my guest to dine me back?
  Of those manners I think not much.

'But you'll pay for your dinner before you depart.
  'Tis hardly fitting or right,
When banqueted so bounteously,
  A yeoman should pay for a knight.'

'Ten shillings is all that my pockets hold,'
  Said the Knight, 'I confess to my shame.'
'By your leave,' said Robin Hood, 'Little John
  Had best have a look all the same.

'If you're telling the truth, not a penny I'll touch,
  For I never plunder the poor;
And if, good sir, you are truly in need,
  Why then, I can lend you more.'

Little John took off his mantle green
  And spread it wide on the ground,
Then emptied the pockets, and when they were bare
  Ten shillings was all he found.

'You have told me the truth. Pour out the best wine,'
  Said Robin. 'Your health, sir! Begin.'
And struck with pity he said, 'I'm amazed
  Your clothes are so ragged and thin.

'Were you forced into knighthood against your will?
  Or have you been false to your wife,
Or squandered your money and lost all your land,
  Or lived with your neighbour in strife?'

'None of this have I done. I was born a knight,'
  He replied. 'And long before,
My ancestors were by heritage knights
  A hundred winters and more.

'My name is Sir Richard of Lee, but alas!
  A man may fall from grace
And suffer distress, till the Lord our God
  Restores him to his place.

'Two years ago I was honoured and rich,
  As all my friends know well;
I had four hundred pound in gold—
  No need my goods to sell.

'But now I have nothing left,' said the Knight,
  'So cruel and harsh is fate.
My wife and children will starve, I fear.
  Your help has come too late.'

'Alas, how did it happen,' said Robin,
  'That all your wealth was lost?'
'Through foolishness and too fond a heart,
  Good sir, I know to my cost.

'I had a son just twenty years old,
    Who would have been my heir.
In the jousting field throughout the land
    He had no match, I swear.

'But he slew a young knight from Lancaster
    And his squire uncouth and bold;
To save his heritage, my goods
    Were forfeited and sold.

'My castle and lands were put in pledge
    Until the settling day;
The Abbot of St. Mary's, York,
    By tomorrow at noon I must pay.'

'What was the sum you borrowed?' said Robin.
    'For how much were you bound?'
'The sum the Abbot lent,' said the Knight,
    'Was just four hundred pound.'

'What will you do if you've lost your lands
    And your debt you cannot pay?'
'I will hasten over the salty sea—
    In England I could not stay—

'Over the sea to Jerusalem,
    Where Jesus lived and died.
Good-bye, my friends. God bless you all.'
    O, heavily he sighed;

And the tears ran streaming down from his eyes.
    ''Tis time I took my course.
Good-bye, my friends. God bless you all.'
    Sadly he turned his horse.

'Wait,' said Robin. 'Have you no friends
    Would help, in charity?'
'Many I had,' said the Knight, 'but now
    They turn their backs on me.

'Once they were proud to welcome me in—
  Now they shut me out in the cold;
They run from me like silly sheep
  Scared by a wolf in the fold.'

'Will none of them stand surety?
  Is there none to lighten your loss?'
'I have no friend,' the Knight replied,
  'Save Christ, who died on the cross.'

'Christ cannot help, I swear by Him
  Who shaped the moon and sun.
Name me a better surety, sir!
  Not a penny you'll get, not one.'

'I can name no other,' the Knight replied,
  'Save Our Lady, to whom I pray.
Never has our dear Lady's help
  Failed me, before today.'

'By Heaven,' said Robin, and crossed himself,
  'If you searched all England through,
You'd not find a better surety—
  I worship our Lady too.

4 THE LOAN

'Go to my treasury, Little John,
  And fetch four hundred pound.'
With Scarlet and Much, John heaped the gold
  In scores and tens on the ground.

'Have you counted right, Little John?' said Much.
  'Four hundred? I make it more.'
'Why should we grudge a few pence? For shame,
  The Knight is perilous poor.

'Pray give him, master, some livery too,
  For his clothes are ragged and thin.
You have red and gold and russet and green
  To wrap his body in.'

'Let him have three yards of every colour,'
  Said Robin, 'and give good measure.'
Little John picked up his brave long-bow.
  'Master,' said he, 'with pleasure.'

He added half a yard to each length.
  Said Much, 'Some draper, I'll say!'
Will Scarlet laughed: 'He has nothing to lose,
  Because he has nothing to pay.'

'Master,' said Little John, 'you can see
  His horse is not sturdy enough.
You must give the Knight a stronger steed
  To carry all this stuff.'

'He shall have my courser grey,' said Robin.
  'The saddle and reins are new.'
'Give him my gloves,' said Will Scarlet,
  'My boots and stockings too.'

Said Robin, 'What will you give him, John,
  That belongs to you, not me?'
'Give him my spurs of silver gilt
  To cheer him up,' said he.

'When shall I pay you back?' said the Knight,
  'And where shall our meeting be?'
'Twelve months from today,' said Robin Hood,
  'Under my trysting tree.

'But it seems to me a shameful thing
  That you, a knight, should ride
With neither yeoman, squire nor page
  To serve you, at your side.

'So Little John shall go with you,
  Let this be now agreed.
He will do you yeoman service, sir,
  If ever you stand in need.'

Said the Knight, 'Your kindness to me's a blessing,
  The best that God has sent.'
He turned his courser into the wood,
  Then away with John he went.

5 AT ST. MARY'S ABBEY

As the Knight was riding with Little John,
  'Listen, good giant,' said he.
'Tomorrow by noon at St. Mary's Abbey
  In York we both must be.

'By noon four hundred pound in gold
  To the Abbot I must pay;
But should I fail, my castle and lands
  Will for ever be taken away.'

The Abbot sat in his cushioned chair;
  His tonsured monks stood round.
'Twelve months ago a Knight came here
  And borrowed four hundred pound.

'If he fails to settle his debt by noon,
  I'll seize his castle and lands,
And the Knight shall be disinherited.'
  He rubbed his greedy hands.

'You are too hasty, sir,' said the Prior.
  'The Knight may arrive here soon.
The sun still climbs on his upward course;
  There's nearly an hour till noon.

'Perchance he has ventured overseas
  In foreign realms to fight,
Enduring many a hungry day
  And many a freezing night.

'Sir Abbot, you'd do him churlish wrong
  His castle and lands to seize
And humble him so shamefully—
  Would that your conscience please?'

'You vex me like a flea in the beard,'
    The Abbot did fret and fume.
A portly monk, the High Cellarer,
    Then lumbered into the room.

'The Knight is slain or hanged,' he said.
    'I'm sure we've nothing to fear.
By the mass, our Abbey stands to gain
    Four hundred pound a year.'

Now the Lord Chief Justice was also there,
    Whom the wily Abbot had paid
To advise him how to sentence the Knight.
    'What think you?' the Abbot said.

Said the pompous Lord, 'He will not come,
    I confidently state.'
But even while the Justice spoke,
    The Knight knocked at the gate.

'Welcome, Sir Knight,' the porter cried.
    'By my beard, though your cheek is lean,
Yours is the finest stallion, sir,
    That I have ever seen.

'Let him be led to the stables now
    To be watered, groomed and fed.'
'Leave him alone. He shall stay with my squire
    By the gate,' Sir Richard said.

6 NO MERCY

Then into the hall Sir Richard stepped,
    In tattered mantle clad,
And knelt at the Abbot's feet, his eyes
    Disconsolate and sad.

'Rejoice with me, Sir Abbot,' he said.
    'I have come to keep my day.'
The first words that the Abbot spoke
    Were, 'Have you brought my pay?'

'Not a penny,' answered the Knight, provoked
    By such discourtesy.
'A devilish debtor you are!' said the Abbot.
    'Sir Justice, drink to me . . .

'If your purse is empty, why have you come,
    Sir Richard? How have you the face?'
Humbly the Knight replied, 'I have come
    To beg for longer grace.'

'If you cannot pay up,' the Justice said,
    'You get no land, God knows.'
'Good Sir Justice, be my friend!
    Protect me from my foes.'

'I am bound to the Abbot,' the Justice said.
    'He pays me with robe and fee.'
'Good Sir Justice, be my friend!'
    'No, by the mass!' said he.

'Good Sir Abbot, be my friend!
    Surely you cannot refuse?
I beseech you, let me keep my lands
    Until I have paid my dues.

'I promise to be your champion true;
    I'll serve you with all my heart,
Until I have saved four hundred pound—
    This very day I'll start.'

The Abbot banged the table and swore,
    'By Him that died on the tree,
Get your land wherever you may!
    You're getting none from me.'

'You refuse to give it me back?' said the Knight.
   'Then heavy shall be my price.
Where is your Christian charity?
   Your heart is cold as ice.'

The Abbot gave him a loathly look.
   'Out, false Knight, from my hall!'
'You lie,' said the Knight. 'I never was false,
   By God that made us all!'

Stiffly, with creaking limbs, he rose.
   'You do me grievous wrong
To shame me so, and, old as I am,
   To make me kneel so long.

'In tournament and joust no man
   More valiantly has fought,
Or for the Faith in foreign realms
   More deadly danger sought.'

'What price, Sir Abbot,' the Justice asked,
   'Would you give for the land's release?
I doubt, unless he be satisfied,
   If you'll hold it long in peace.'

'A hundred pound,' said the Abbot, 'no more.'
   Said the Justice, 'Give him two.'
'No, by Heaven!' Sir Richard cried,
   'I will not haggle with you.

'Though you offered me a thousand more,
   I'd sell you no land, I swear.
Abbot, Justice, friar or monk
   Never shall be my heir.'

'Out of my hall, sir! Must I call
   My man?' the Abbot said.
'Save your saintly breath,' said the Knight.
   'I will call *my* man instead.'

He raised his horn to his lips and blew.
  With a mighty clap on the door,
Little John like a monster hound
  Came lolloping over the floor.

Out of the mouth of his leather bag
  And on to the table round,
Among plate and platter and silver cup
  He poured four hundred pound.

'Sir Abbot, here is your gold,' said John.
  'Reach out and help yourself.'
As the golden coins came clattering down,
  The Abbey clock struck twelve.

'Had you been courteous,' said the Knight,
  'I'd have added a gift for the loan.'
The Abbot stared, he said not a word,
  He sat as still as stone.

At last he said, with a ponderous sigh,
  'Sir Justice, take your fee.'
'Not a penny I'll touch. As the Knight has paid,
  I give my service free.'

'Sir Abbot, and masters of law,' said the Knight,
  'I was true. I kept my day:
My land is my own again by right,
  Whatever you think or say.

'Come, good squire, 'tis time we were gone.
  Away with worry and care!'
He put on his russet mantle and tossed
  The tattered cloak on a chair.

Then, singing merrily, off he rode,
  And soon (so goes the tale)
His Lady greeted him at the gate
  Of his home in Wyersdale.

'Welcome, my lord, O welcome!' she said.
  'Did you lose your land today?'
'Rejoice, my love. It is mine again,
  And for Robin Hood we'll pray.

'God bless him, bring his soul to bliss!
  He raised me up from sorrow.
Without his bounty, we'd have starved
  And beggars been tomorrow.

'The Abbot and I have made our peace;
  I've returned the gold he lent.
In a year I'll pay good Robin back,
  When I've saved my tenants' rent.'

In three months John returned to the wood
  With his master Robin to stay;
But Sir Richard tarried at home in peace
  To wait for the reckoning day.

Then a hundred bows of yew he brought,
  All strung and corded tight,
And a hundred sheaf of peacock arrows,
  Their tips all burnished bright.

He loaded the gifts on a baggage mule,
  And a hundred guards went too,
As, lance in hand, in scarlet clad,
  The woods he cantered through.

By a bridge he came to a wrestling match;
  Through the jostling crowd he pressed,
Then watched for a while the champions vie
  With a stranger come from the west.

The prize was no ram but a snow-white bull,
  A ring that did glitter and shine,
Grey gloves, a stallion bridled and saddled,
  And a barrel of blood-red wine.

Sir Richard marked how the stranger threw
  Each challenger that came;
But friendless he was—when the crowd attacked,
  The stranger was nearly slain.

How he pitied the lad, for brave was he
  As alone he parried the blows.
'For the love of Robin Hood,' said the Knight,
  'I'll save him from his foes.'

His hundred guards then bent their bows,
    Each drew to the ear his string.
'Leave him alone,' Sir Richard cried,
    'Or you'll hear these arrows sing!'

The cowards fell back and made room for the Knight,
    To listen to what he'd say.
Clasping the stranger's hand, he cried,
    'Sir, you have won the day.

'Here's five marks for the wine. I care not
    What these champions think—
Take your prize, sir, broach the barrel!
    All here your health shall drink.'

He tarried until the match was done,
    Then left the field at last . . .
But Robin had eaten nothing still—
    And three hours from noon had passed.

9 THE NEWCOMERS

'' Tis time we ate our dinner,' said John.
  But Robin Hood said, 'Nay.
Sir Richard should have arrived by noon—
  Today is his reckoning day.'

'Fear not, master,' said Little John.
  'The sun is not yet to rest,
And of all the knights in Christendom
  Sir Richard's truest and best.'

'But a man must eat and drink,' said Robin,
  'To brave the greenwood weather.
Were it the King of England, John,
  I could not wait for ever.

'Take Scarlet and Much and, bow in hand,
  Walk to Watling Street,
And wait there under the trees until
  Some guest you chance to meet.

'Whether he be King's messenger
  Or minstrel, singer of songs;
If he be poor, whatever of mine
  He needs, to him belongs.'

So John and Scarlet and Much went off,
  A little dismayed and vexed,
With broadswords under their Lincoln green . . .
  Now hear what happened next.

Straightway they walked to Watling Street,
  Those sturdy yeomen three;
They looked to the east, they looked to the west,
  But nobody could they see.

But as they looked down Barnsley Dale
    Along the highway-side,
They were aware of two black monks
    On trotting nags astride.

'Loosen your swords,' said Little John.
    'Look to your bows, I say,
And string your arrows. I'll wager my life
    Those monks have brought my pay;

'For two-and-fifty guards, I see,
    Their seven mules surround.
In all the land no bishop rides
    So royally, I'll be bound.'

'And we are only three,' said Much.
    'I fear we'll meet disgrace.
Unless we bring those monks to dinner,
    Our master we dare not face.'

'Bend your bows,' said John. 'By my beard,
    That monk that leads their band,
I met him at St. Mary's Abbey.
    His life is in my hand.

'Stay, you churlish monk,' he cried,
    'Or this arrow I'll let fly.
You have kept my master waiting, sir.
    One step, and you shall die!'

'Who is your master?' asked the monk.
    'His name is Robin Hood.'
'A wicked thieving knave,' said the monk,
    'Of whom I have heard no good.'

'False monk, you lie!' said Little John.
    'Those words you'll soon forget,
When you've dined with him in the woods today
    And you and he have met.'

Then Much prodded the monk with his bow.
   Said the monk, 'Hands off, I say!'
As he slid from his horse to the ground, his fellow
   Spurred through the woods away.

The others scattered like leaves in the wind;
   All two-and-fifty fled,
Save for a page-boy and a groom—
   With John two mules they led.

10 SOUR AS VINEGAR

They brought the monk to the trysting tree,
   Resentful, unresigned,
And mouthing curses all the way,
   While the mules were dragged behind.

Politely Robin bared his head;
   But the monk pulled down his cowl
With trembling hand, to hood his eyes
   And hide his angry scowl.

'He's sour as vinegar,' said John.
   Said Robin, 'Not worth your heeding.
Discourtesy I hate and scorn.
   He has no birth or breeding.

'But did he bring no guards with him?
   How came he here alone?'
'There were two-and-fifty when we met,
   And now, like birds, they've flown.'

'Let me blow my horn,' said Robin Hood.
   'My men shall meet our guest.'
He blew, and seven score yeomen sprang
   From north, south, east and west,

Each in his summer suit of gold
    And russet bravely clad,
With bow and trusty blade and mantle
    Striped with scarlet red.

They forced the monk to wash his hands
    And dry them, flabby, gleaming,
Then sit by the crackling fire where pots
    Of venison were steaming.

'Eat well,' said Robin. With his greedy eyes
    And dappled lobster cheeks,
The monk gobbled his food—you'd guess
    He'd eaten none for weeks.

'What is your Abbey and office?' said Robin.
    'And how do you spend your time?'
'In the cellars of St. Mary's, York,
    I look to the ale and wine.'

'High Cellarer, I welcome you.
    You are rich, and wine is your wealth.
Fill up his cup with the best we have—
    This monk shall drink my health.

'Good cheer I need, for my mind has been
    Troubled and vexed all day;
I fear Our Lady is angry with me—
    She has brought me not my pay.'

'Now the monk has come from Her Abbey,' said John,
    'No need to worry and fret.
He has brought it with him, master. I swear
    You'll have your money yet.'

'Our Lady,' said Robin, 'stood surety
    Between a poor Knight and me.
I lent him a sum of money here
    Under the greenwood tree.

'If you've brought it back, then show us the gold
    And John shall count it through;
And should you ever need help, God grant
    I may do as much for you.'

The monk he swore a mighty oath
    And cried out, 'This is absurd!
Of the loan you draw my attention to
    Not a whisper have I heard.'

'But you are Our Lady's messenger
    From the Abbey that bears her name,
And a Knight that puts his trust in Her
    Can never be brought to shame.

'What have you, sir, in your saddle-bags?'
    Said Robin. 'Now tell me true.'
'Sir,' said the monk, 'I've twenty marks
    To see my journey through.'

'If that is all,' said Robin, 'I swear
    I will not touch one penny;
And willingly I'll lend you more,
    If you are needing any.

'But if you have lied to me, sir monk,
    Your deceit shall cost you dear.
Little John, go and search his bags
    And bring me the money here.'

John spread his cloak upon the ground,
    As he'd done so often before;
In piles of silver and gold he poured
    Eight hundred pound and more.

Loud he laughed, and to Robin he ran
    And stood at his side in a trice.
'He is truly Our Lady's messenger,
    This monk—She has paid you twice.'

'What did I tell you?' said Robin. 'Sir monk,
    If you searched all England through,
You could fare no better. As surety,
    Our Lady's the best I know.

'Fill up the goblets! The monk shall drink.
    Our Lady is gracious and kind.
If She ever needs help from Robin Hood,
    A friend in him She will find.

'And should She need more silver and gold,
    Again to me She must come;
And, by this token She's given today,
    She may have three times the sum.

'But why did you risk so much, sir monk?
    Did you reckon for treacherous reeves,
For robbers and sheriffs that ride the roads,
    For thickets that bristle with thieves?'

'The gold,' said the monk, 'was a gift from my house
  To the King at Westminster court.'
He lied; he rode there to humble the Knight—
  A judge with gold could be bought.

'Does the second mule carry gold for the King?'
  Said Robin. 'Let John go and see.'
'By the bones of the saints,' the High Cellarer cried,
  'Do you call it courtesy

'To kidnap a guest, then use him as prey
  To plunder and beat and bind?'
''Tis an old custom of ours,' said Robin,
  'To leave very little behind.'

The cowardly monk clapped spurs to his horse—
  He had no taste for staying.
'Won't you stop for a drink ere you go?' called Robin.
  'It might inspire your praying.'

'No!' cried the monk. 'And a curse on my folly,
  That ever I ventured here!
Alas, how much cheaper my dinner had been
  In Blyth or Doncaster!'

'Greet your Abbot from me,' said Robin,
  'Your Prior as well, I say;
And ask him to send me a monk like you
  To dine with every day.'

11 THE RECKONING

Now let us say no more of the monk,
  But speak of the gentle Knight.
He sped through the wood till Robin he reached
  In the last of the evening light.

Lightly down from his horse he leapt,
　And joyful was their meeting.
Robin bowed, then doffed his hood
　And bent his knee in greeting.

'Welcome, sir Knight. What brings you here,
　And why have you dallied so long?'
'The Abbot fought hard to keep the lands
　That by right to me belong.'

'But have you bought them back again?
　Sir Richard, tell me true.'
'They are mine at last, by the grace of God
　And thanks, good Robin, to you.

'Forgive me, sir, that I dallied so long—
　Some wrestlers came to blows;
I rescued a yeoman sore beset
　And freed him from his foes.'

'Forgive?' said Robin. 'But you did well,
　And I would blame you never;
The man who helps a yeoman in need
　Remains my friend for ever.'

'I have brought four hundred pound,' said the Knight,
　'The money you lent to me,
And a gift of twenty marks, kind sir,
　For your thought and courtesy.'

'Keep your money. You owe me nothing.
　The settlement has been made:
Our Lady, through the High Cellarer,
　With interest has paid.

'But were I to take the money twice,
　I would hide my head in shame;
So I welcome you with all my heart,
　Sir Knight, and bless your name.'

Then Robin told him all, and Sir Richard
  Laughed both loud and long.
'But take this money, I beg you, sir;
  To you it must belong.'

'I protest, you owe me nothing,' said Robin.
  'Keep it and use it well,
To dress your lady in finest silk
  And your empty coffers swell.

'But what are these hundred bows of yew
    All strung and corded tight,
And these hundred sheaf of peacock arrows,
    Their tips all burnished bright?'

'My humble gifts to you,' said the Knight,
    'Your pleasure and joy to earn.'
'By the mass,' said Robin, 'such courtesy
    Deserves a rich return.

'Go to my treasury, Little John,
    And fetch four hundred pound—
The money the Cellarer overpaid—
    And count it out on the ground.

'You shall buy a cloak, sir, trimmed with fur,
    A horse and harness too,
And deck your shield with glittering gems
    And gild your spurs anew.

'But should you fall on evil days
    And Robin's help can avail,
Hasten home to the good greenwood—
    His bounty never will fail.'

'If ever it lie in my power,' said the Knight,
    'Your kindness I will repay.'
And, mounting his horse, with his hundred guards
    He rode through the woods away.

A Sackful of Silver

I AT THE SHOOTING BUTTS

I'll tell you a tale of Little John,
   How he left Sir Richard of Lee
To serve as the Sheriff's man, and how
   He returned to the greenwood tree.

One day the merry young men made haste
   To the butts their skill to try;
Little John went too, and the proud Sheriff
   Of Nottingham stood by.

Three times Little John let go the string,
    Three times he slit the wand.
'He's a champion archer,' the Sheriff declared,
    'The finest in all the land.

'Come over here, young fellow,' he called.
    'Now tell me, what is your name
And where do you live? And tell me too
    The country whence you came.'

'My mother,' said John, 'once told me, sir,
    That in Holderness I was born.
Ronald Greenleaf they call me at home,
    'Tis a name no man will scorn.'

'Ronald Greenleaf,' the Sheriff said,
    'Are you willing to work for me?
I'll feed and clothe you, and twenty marks
    A year your pay shall be.'

'I serve a master,' said Little John,
    'A courteous Knight and true;
But if he will release me, sir,
    I'll gladly go with you.'

To release Little John for a year
    The Knight was pleased to arrange;
And the Sheriff gave him a stallion, strong
    And sturdy, in exchange.

So John became the Sheriff's man;
    But you must not think him mad,
For he planned to be the worst servant
    The Sheriff ever had.

2 THE KITCHEN BRAWL

One Wednesday when the Sheriff was out
  A-hunting over the hill,
Little John lay long in bed—
  At noon he was sleeping still.

The Sheriff he had forgotten him,
  And when he woke at mid-day,
'Give me my dinner, steward,' he called,
  'For the breakfast's cleared away.'

'I'll give you nothing,' the steward growled,
  'Till my lord is back in town.'
'If that is the case,' said Little John,
  'I've a mind to crack your crown.

'Give me my dinner, butler,' he called,
  'And a bottle of wine from the store.'
'You'll get no dinner from me,' said the butler,
  And banged the buttery door.

Little John kicked the door from its hinge;
  One leap and he was through.
He hit the butler's back so hard
  It nearly broke in two.

Then Little John ate and Little John drank;
  And to show how he liked to dine,
He swallowed a trayful of raspberry tarts
  And washed them down with wine.

'What a ravenous fellow you are!' said the cook.
  'You know how to drink and eat.'
And with his powdered rolling-pin
  He knocked him clean from his seat.

He drew his sword and John drew his,
  And into the fray they dashed;
Up and down the kitchen floor
  For a mile or two they clashed.

'Enough!' cried John. 'Put up your sword!
  Such skill I'll never forget.
You're one of the finest swordsmen, sir,
  That I have ever met.

'If you'd like to shoot as well with the bow,
  Then follow the greenwood track
And come with me, and you shall earn
  Two suits a year to your back.

'And Robin Hood will give you each year
    Twenty marks in pay.'
'Agreed,' said the cook, and sheathed his sword.
    'Now let's be friends, I say.'

They feasted then on venison,
    With wine both red and white.
'We'll away to the wood to Robin Hood,'
    They vowed, 'this very night.'

3 THE MASTER HART

They ran to the Sheriff's treasury
    And smashed the iron locks;
Three hundred pound in gold they seized
    From chest and money-box.

They filled a sack with silver vessels,
    As many as they could find;
Goblet, chalice, cup or spoon—
    Nothing was left behind.

Then off they rode to the good greenwood.
    'God bless you, master dear,'
Said Little John. Said Robin Hood,
    'You are most welcome here.

'Welcome too is your yeoman friend—
    Good cooks we never refuse;
And since you have come from Nottingham town,
    Tell me, John, the news.'

'The Sheriff sends his greetings, master,
    A handsome present too—
His cook and all his silverware,
    And three hundred pound, for you.'

U. S. 1535276

'I'll take my oath,' said Robin Hood,
  'By all the saints above,
He never sent these gifts to me
  Through heart-felt Christian love.'

Then Little John, in a twinkling, thought
  Of a shrewd and cunning plan.
'Good-bye!' he called, then away through the wood
  Five panting miles he ran.

At last he came up with the proud Sheriff,
  A-hunting with horn and hound.
He leapt from his horse, bowed courteously,
  Then knelt at his feet on the ground.

'At last I've caught you, master,' he gasped,
    Breathless with pursuing.
'Ronald Greenleaf, where have you been
    And what have you been doing?'

'While walking through the forest, sir,
    A wondrous sight I saw—
A master hart with leaf-green hide
    And a herd of seven score.

'Their antlers are so piercing sharp
    They made me shake with fear;
I dared not lift my brave long-bow
    And shoot, or venture near.'

'I'd part with all my silverware,'
    Said the Sheriff, 'that sight to see.'
'—if you'd any silver left,' said John.
    'Come quickly. Follow me.'

The Sheriff rode and Little John ran
    Deep into the wood.
'Here is your master hart,' said John,
    Pointing at Robin Hood.

4 'WILL YOU JOIN OUR GREENWOOD ORDER?'

Still as stone the Sheriff stood,
    A sorry man was he.
'Ronald Greenleaf, you've played me false,
    But you'll pay for your treachery.'

'As God is my witness, Sheriff,' said John,
    ''Tis you must bear the blame.
I could get no dinner in your house,
    So back to the woods I came.'

The Sheriff sat down. The silverware
  On the table glittered bright;
But when he saw whose silver it was,
  He lost his appetite.

'Come, make yourself at home,' said Robin,
  'Here are your spoon and knife.
Cheer up! For love of Little John,
  I mean to spare your life.'

When supper was done—'Take off his boots
  And stockings,' Robin said.
'The sun went down long since,' he yawned.
  'The Sheriff's ready for bed.'

They took off his boots and stockings, his coat
  And gown of satin sheen;
Tight as a babe they swaddled him
  In cloth of Lincoln green.

The Sheriff lay shivering all night long
  In his breeches and silken shirt;
He woke in the morning stiff and numb—
  Whenever he moved, it hurt.

'Will you join our Greenwood Order,' said Robin,
  'And share our sport and mirth?'
''Tis too severe. I wouldn't stay here
  For all the gold on earth.'

'You'd soon pick up our lawless ways.
  Do stay with us,' Robin said.
'I'd die of cold. I'd rather swing,'
  Said the Sheriff, 'or lose my head.

'O, Robin, let me go!' he whined.
  'I promise my ways to mend;
And you shall find in Nottingham town
  You have no better friend.'

'Then swear me an oath,' said Robin Hood,
  'With my bright sword in your hand,
That you'll never seek to do me harm
  By water or by land.

'And if you find any man of mine,
  Whether by night or day,
You'll give me your word of honour, sir,
  To help him as best you may.'

The Sheriff swore the oath, but his heart
  Was smouldering with hate;
And he galloped home on his dapple,grey
  A chance of revenge to wait.

The Sheriff's Revenge

I THE SILVER ARROW

'Listen,' the proud Sheriff cried,
    'And hearken to what I say.
A shooting-match I now proclaim
    For next midsummer day.
Let the bravest archers come, and the best
    Shall bear the prize away.

'A costly arrow shall he win,
    With shaft of silver white
And feathers and tip of rich red gold—
    'Tis lightning-swift in flight.'

When Robin heard this joyful news
    Under his trysting tree,
'Get ready, get ready, my merry young men,
    We'll go to the butts,' said he,
'And whether the Sheriff honours his oath,
    I vow, we soon shall see.'

They looked to their feathers, they bent their bows;
    And when all their tackle was trim,
Full seven score of his merry young men
    Marched through the woods with him.

And when they came to Nottingham town,
    Long were the butts and fair,
And many an arrow from twanging string
    Went whizzing through the air.

'Six of you now will shoot,' said Robin.
    'The rest at hand shall stay.
So hide you here with your good bows bent,
    For fear there be foul play.'

Three yeomen then their arrows let fly;
    The fourth was Robin Hood.
The Sheriff he watched him draw the string—
    Alert by the butts he stood.

Three times did Robin shoot, three times
    He slit the willow wand;
Then Scarlet grazed it, so did John
    And Gilbert of the white hand;
But Ronald missed by a finger's breadth,
    And Much hit a branch beyond.

Never before had the Sheriff beheld
    A contest half as good;
But of all who bent their bows that day
    The best was Robin Hood.

'The prize is justly won,' said the Sheriff.
    'Take it, sir, and depart.'
His words were fair but his smile was false,
    For treason blackened his heart.

When Robin had thanked him courteously,
    To the woods he turned to go,
But the Sheriff suddenly raised a shout
    And the horns began to blow.

'Shame on you, Sheriff!' cried Robin. 'O, shame!
    Is it thus you greet your guest?
These arrows you aim at us, are they
    The prize that you professed?'

With hail of arrows the Sheriff's men
    Those scornful words defied,
And many a bow was bent and many
    A shaft did glance and glide;
And many a coat was ripped and rent,
    And pierced was many a side.

But when the quivers were empty, lo!
    'Twas the Sheriff's men lay dead;
And their cowardly fellows, to save their skins,
    Turned on their heels and fled.

2 REFUGE

Little John was wounded sore
    With an arrow stuck in his knee.
Alas! he could neither walk nor ride,
    It hurt so grievously.

'Master, for Jesus' sake,' he said,
    'If ever I served you well,
Kill me quickly—I have no taste
    For the Sheriff's dungeon cell.

'I fear he'll return and find me here—
    I beg you, strike off my head,
Or plunge your dagger into my breast,
    And leave me here for dead.'

'I love you with all my heart,' said Robin.
    'Dear giant, understand
I would not have you slain, I vow,
    For all the gold in the land.'

'By Heaven,' said Much, 'not one of us here
    Would take your life today.'
But Little John heard never a word,
    For he'd fainted clean away.

Then Much he lifted him on to his back
    And carried him many a mile;
Sometimes he paused to use his bow
    And ward off foes the while.

At last they came to a courtly castle
    Beside a hazel wood,
With a moat all round; the rugged walls
    Much battering had withstood.

This was the home of a noble Knight,
    The same Sir Richard of Lee
Whom Robin had lent four hundred pound
    Under the greenwood tree.
He welcomed Robin into his hall
    With all his company.

'Good Robin, of all the men in the world
    I swear I love you most.
To return your trust and courtesy,
    I'll joyfully be your host.

'Shut the gates and draw up the bridge,
    Prepare to parry attack;
Arm yourselves to the hilt, I say,
    And we'll drive the Sheriff back.

'We'll drive him back, we'll strike him down,
    And by St. Quintin I swear
For forty days you'll be my guest
    And feast on royal fare.

'Let the cloth be spread, the table laid!
    Bring in the ale and wine!
As I drink your health, forget your cares.
    Sit down, my friends, and dine.'

3 'I'LL GO TO THE KING'

Full fast the Sheriff of Nottingham
    Summoned his army out,
Laid siege at once to the castle walls
    And packed his men about.

'Ho there!' the haughty Sheriff cried.
    'Do you hear me, traitor Knight?
You shield King Edward's enemy
    Against all lawful right.'

'Myself I'll answer for what I have done,'
    Sir Richard of Lee replied.
'My lands and castle I hold from the King—
    Both clear of debt, untied.

'As for my guests, 'tis not to you
    But the King I must speak out.
You should ask his leave at Westminster,
    If you seek my rights to flout.'

'Then I'll go to the King,' the Sheriff said.
    'I'll plead my case to the Crown.'
And mounting his dapple-grey, hot haste,
    He spurred to London town.

'Robin has slain your deer, my Liege,
  And slighted the forest laws;
And now Sir Richard of Lee holds court
  To these mutinous outlaws.'

'I will go to Nottingham,' said the King,
  'To set this matter right;
Robin I'll make my prisoner
  And silence the stubborn Knight.

'Go home, good Sheriff, and do as I bid.
  Go home at once,' said he,
'And summon all the bowmen you may
  From over the north country.'

When the Sheriff rode home into Nottingham town,
    Full forty days had passed;
And Robin Hood and his merry men
    Had returned to the woods at last.

And Little John was healed of his hurt,
    The arrow plucked from his knee;
And Robin Hood had welcomed him back
    Under the greenwood tree.

But sore was the Sheriff he couldn't lay hands
    On Robin and pounce on his prey;
So he lay in wait for the gentle Knight
    And watched for him night and day.

He was hawking by the riverside,
    Gentle Sir Richard of Lee,
A hooded falcon perched on his wrist.
    As he set the falcon free,

The Sheriff's men sprang at his throat
    And hurled him hard to the ground,
Then carried him off to Nottingham town,
    In ropes and fetters bound.
'Were it Robin instead,' the Sheriff he said,
    'I'd give one hundred pound.'

4 ROBIN TO THE RESCUE

When Sir Richard's lady heard how it was,
    She saddled her chestnut mare
And galloped alone to the good greenwood
    And met with Robin there.

'God bless you, Robin, and all your men.
    I come not a minute too soon.
For our dear Lady's sake, good Robin,
    I beg you to grant me a boon.

'O let not the lord I wedded and love
   Shamefully be slain!
He's been carried away to Nottingham town,
   And the proud Sheriff's to blame.'

'The Sheriff, you say?' cried Robin. 'By Heaven,
   I have waited long for this chance.
Which way did he pass? How far has he gone?
   I swear I'll lead him a dance.'

'Three miles or less he's ridden, sir.
   You've time to overtake.
I fear he will murder my lord—O, Robin,
   Run, for our Lady's sake!'

Up sprang Robin; his eyes were wild,
   And lightning-fierce his face.
'Make ready, make ready, my merry young men!
   We must the Sheriff outpace.

'The man who takes no heed of this sorrow,
   By Him that died on the cross,
Shall dwell no more in the woods with me,
   And I will not mourn his loss.'

They filled their quivers, they grasped their bows,
   Not a yeoman would stand disgraced.
Over hedge and ditch, through thicket and copse
   Fleet as the wind they raced.

'As God above is my witness,' said Robin,
   'The haughty Sheriff I'll catch.
He will not trouble us more, I swear.
   This time he will meet his match.'

They caught up the Sheriff at Nottingham gate—
  He was prancing, puffed with pride,
With Sir Richard (his mantle muddied and torn)
  Sad and pale at his side;
His hands were bound like a thief's, his feet
  Under his horse were tied.

'Halt, proud Sheriff,' cried Robin, 'and speak,
  For I know you've come from the King.
I'm eager to hear what tidings he sent.
  Tell me, what news do you bring?

'By Heaven,' he panted, 'these seven long years
  I have not run so fast.
But why do your fingers reach for your sword?
  And why do you look downcast?'

Then Robin bent his strong yew-bow,
  He drew the string with a will;
The flint-head winged to its mark, and the Sheriff
  Slumped to the ground and lay still.

Before he could reel to his feet and fly,
  Bold Robin toward him sped;
He snatched from the scabbard his nut-brown sword
  And smote off the Sheriff's head.

'Lie there, lie there, proud Sheriff,' he cried,
  'And keep your tryst with the dust.
Merciless, false and cruel were you,
  A brute no man could trust.'

His merry young men then drew their swords,
  That were so sharp and keen;
They soon disposed of the Sheriff's men—
  Not one was to be seen.

Then Robin ran to the noble Knight,
    Untied each foot and hand.
'Take hold of this strong yew-bow,' he cried,
    'Step down from the saddle and stand.

'Leave your horse and trust to your feet;
    Stand up and do not tire.
You shall run with me to the good greenwood
    Through fen and moss and mire,

'And dwell there under the cheerful sky
    Where thrush and blackbird sing,
Until I have my pardon won
    From Edward, our comely King.'

The King's Pardon

I 'I'LL HANG THAT TRAITOR'

King Edward rode to Nottingham town
　　With barons in royal array,
To capture the Knight and Robin Hood;
　　And he asked for them on his way.

But when he heard how the Sheriff was slain
　　By Robin Hood and his band,
How the gentle Knight was in league with them,
　　He seized Sir Richard's land.

Through the valleys and hills of Lancashire
   He journeyed far and near,
Until he came to Plumpton Park,
   Where he loved to hunt the deer.

For towering antlers, bounding herds
   In vain the King did look;
In Plumpton Park he could scarcely find
   A single stag or buck.

The King was wondrously enraged;
    He swore by yea and nay,
'I'll hang that traitor Robin Hood—
    O, would he were here today!

'The man who brings me Sir Richard's head
    Shall be lord of all his land;
He shall have the deed and document
    Sealed by my royal hand.'

Then up and spoke a white-haired baron:
    ''Twill do him little good.
The lord of Sir Richard's land, my Liege,
    Must reckon with Robin Hood.

'While Robin Hood still walks and rides
    And holds a bow in his hand,
Death is the only gift bestowed—
    What use Sir Richard's land?'

The King he dwelt in Nottingham town
    For more than half a year;
And yet of Robin Hood and his men
    Not a single word did he hear.

But free as the wind went Robin Hood
    By heath and valley and hill;
He cared not a fig for the forest laws,
    He slew the deer at will.

2 IN DISGUISE

Then up and spoke a forester,
    That stood at the King's right knee:
'If you would set eyes on Robin Hood,
    My Liege, pay heed to me.

'Gather five of your faithful knights
    And set out, as I advise,
To yonder abbey, and clothe yourselves
    At once in monks' disguise.

'Then follow me through woodland ways
    —I'll be your trusty guide—
And by all the Saints I swear you'll meet
    With Robin, if he's alive.'

King Edward chose five faithful knights;
    Hotfoot they hurried away,
And at the abbey clothed themselves
    In cowls of convent grey.

With an abbot's cloak, stiff riding-boots,
    And a broad-brimmed hat on his crown,
He led his five grey-hooded monks
    Through the streets of Nottingham town,

Then out to the woods with the forester's help
    Bold Robin Hood to find;
And the King was humming a sprightly tune,
    While the pack-mules followed behind.

They had scarcely ridden a mile, a mile,
    When into the greenwood track
Leapt Robin Hood, with five and thirty
    Bowmen at his back.

Then seizing hold of the King's bridle,
    'By your leave, Sir Abbot,' said he,
'You and your monks must now dismount
    And tarry awhile with me.'

'You startled my horse with your noisy din.
    Who are you?' King Edward said.
'We are yeomen who live in the woods, Sir Abbot,
    And deer are our daily bread.

'But *you* have churches and land and rent,
    Warm clothes and money in plenty.
Give us your gold. For each fat-bellied monk,
    Of the starving poor there are twenty.'

'Alas, I have brought but forty pound,'
    Said the King, 'and as for the rest,
I have spent it all these two weeks past
    While I stayed with the King as guest.
But had I a hundred pound, 'twould be yours
    To give the poor and oppressed.'

Robin Hood then took the gold
    And gladly gave it away,
Half to his men, and half to the Abbot
    To keep till another day.

'Our grateful thanks,' the Abbot said.
    'I have greetings here from our King.
He bids you to dine in Nottingham town—
    His letter and seal I bring.'

He took out the parchment and, breaking the seal,
    Unrolled it for Robin to see.
'I love no man as much as my King,'
    Said Robin, and dropped to his knee.

Then lightly Robin leapt to his feet
    And led the King by the hand;
And many a dainty deer was slain
    And a tasty banquet planned.

He pressed his bugle-horn to his lips,
    A mighty blast he blew;
And seven score of his merry young men
    Burst the branches through.

They knelt to Robin. 'By Heaven,' said the King,
    'This is a wondrous sight.
I wish my men when I bade them come
    Were half as prompt and polite.'

The feast was made ready, the table set,
    And the King sat down to dine;
And Robin Hood and giant John
    They served him, two at a time,
With venison, fine white bread, brown ale,
    And flagons of blood-red wine.

3 A GAME OF PLUCK-BUFFET

When the feast was finished, the merry young men
    Leapt up and bent their bows.
'See how well they can shoot,' said Robin.
    With fear King Edward froze.

For a game of 'pluck-buffet' they set two wands
    In the grass, then marched to their places.
'But the wands are too far away,' said the King,
    'Too far by fifty paces.'

With a garland of roses they crowned each wand—
    Targets true and clear.
'The man who misses his mark,' said Robin,
    'Shall forfeit all his gear

'And surrender it to his master, who—
    Such sport will we provide—
Shall reward him for his marksmanship
    And buffet him, head and side.'

Twice did Robin bend his bow,
    And twice he slit the wand;
And so did Arthur a-Bland and Much
    And Gilbert of the white hand.

But Little John and Scarlet they missed
    By fingers three and four;
So they gave their gear to Robin Hood,
    Who smote them wondrous sore—
Then drew the last of his arrows and missed
    By half a span and more.

Then said Gilbert of the white hand,
    'Master, your gear is lost.
Your bow and arrows they both are mine.
    Stand fast and pay the cost.'

'If that is the case,' said Robin Hood,
    'I'll give my arrows and bow
To *you*, Sir Abbot. Give me the buffet.'
    He knelt to receive the blow.

''Tis against the rules of my order, Robin,
    To use my strong right arm
To smite a yeoman. Forgive me, sir.
    I might do grievous harm.'

'Smite on,' said Robin. 'I'm not afraid.
    Gladly I give you leave.'
'Then take whatever comes,' said the King;
    And, rolling up his sleeve,

He gave poor Robin a desperate blow—
    He was felled like a tree to the ground.
'By Heaven, there's strength in your arm!' cried Robin.
    'Some friar, I'll be bound!

'How well can you shoot?'—'I can shoot as well
    As your King,' the Abbot he said.
And flinging away his hat and cowl,
    He bared his comely head.

'I am your King,' the Abbot confessed,
   As Robin dropped to his knee.
'Be merciful, Robin. We're in your power.
   Protect my men and me.'

'By St. Mary, I will,' said Robin Hood.
   'I'm your host and subject too!
'Tis I who must for my men and me
   Crave pardon, my Liege, from you.'

'I'll grant it gladly, sir, if you'll quit
    Your merry greenwood sport
And return to my palace at Westminster
    And live with me at court.'

'In your service, my Liege, at Westminster,
    My days will be nobly spent,
If Little John and my seven score men
    May join us, with your consent.'
'Take whoever you will,' said the King.
    'Good Robin, I'm well content.'

4 ON THE MARCH

'Have you any green cloth for me and my monks,'
    Said the King, 'you would sell to me?'
'Indeed I have, my Liege,' said Robin.
    'I've thirty yards and three.'

They clothed themselves in Lincoln green,
    They cast aside their grey.
'And now we must ride to Nottingham town,'
    Said the King. 'We'll leave today.'

'Trim your arrows and bend your bows
    For a shooting-match in the wood.'
Many a buffet King Edward won
    That day from Robin Hood.

'By Heaven,' laughed the King, 'this game
    Is too hard to learn, I fear;
I never could win a buffet on you,
    Though I practised all the year.'

The people of Nottingham watched them come,
    They were terror-struck by the scene—
From rim to rim of the sky a marching
    Meadow of Lincoln green.

Then every man to his neighbour stammered,
　'I fear our King is slain.
If Robin attacks, we'll none of us live
　To see the morrow again.

'We must steal from hearth and home and run
　Ere Robin starts his tricks.'
And away they fled—the crippled and lame
　Went hobbling on their sticks.

The King looked on, and loud he laughed:
 'We have no mind to attack.
Stop, my friends! Turn home!' he cried.
 And they all came hobbling back.

He called for gentle Sir Richard of Lee
 And gave him back his land,
Then returned to his palace at Westminster
 With Robin Hood and his band.

5 THE PALACE OF WESTMINSTER

When Robin had dwelt in Westminster
 For twelve months and a day,
All his band but Scarlet and John,
 Like his money, had melted away.

He chanced one day on a shooting-match.
 As the winged arrows sped,
'These brave young men, how true their aim!
 They'll surpass me soon,' he said.
'I was once the finest shot in the land,
 But alas, my skill is fled.

'At Westminster I wither away,
 In the musty court I choke.
O for the greenwood, where at dawn
 With the early thrush I woke!'

Then Robin went to the King. 'My Liege,
 A boon I beg,' said he.
'I built a chapel in Barnsley Dale,
 And it's there I long to be.

'Believe me, Sire, for seven long nights
 I have not slept a wink;
For seven long days so ill was I,
 I could neither eat nor drink.

'But my chapel at Barnsley Dale will give me
 The balm my spirit needs.
Barefoot, ragged I've vowed to go
 To atone for my misdeeds.'

'Seven days I'll grant, no more,' said the King.
 'Seven days, 'tis long to part.
Take Scarlet and John. But I'll miss you all—
 You're yeomen after my heart.'

'O, thank you, thank you, my bounteous Lord,'
 Said Robin, on bended knee.
Most courteously he took his leave;
 To the greenwood hastened he.

6 UNDER THE GREENWOOD TREE

'Twas the month of May, and the turtle dove
 Soft in the wood did sing.
As Robin under the branches walked,
 His merry voice chimed in
With blackbird, cuckoo, linnet and thrush—
 O, loud did the woodland ring.

'Look,' said Scarlet. 'In brake and copse
 The swarthy ash-bud swells.'
'Breathe deep,' said giant John, 'and taste
 How sweet the hawthorn smells.'

'An age has passed,' said Robin Hood,
 'Since last we revelled here.
How I long to grasp my strong yew-bow
 And try my skill with the deer!'

Then Robin he slew a tall-antlered buck;
 Will Scarlet dressed it fine;
John roasted it; and then they supped
 And washed it down with wine.

The sun went down, the moon uprose,
    And John and Scarlet slept;
But Robin lay wide awake; he mused
    As the purple shadows crept:

'I have no money, I have no men
    But these my faithful two.'
With a sudden bound he leapt to his feet,
    Then raised his horn and blew;
And away and away through the ghostly glades
    The ghostly echoes flew.

Seven score yeomen heard that note;
    They knew it and came right soon;
They came in raiment ragged and torn
    As the clouds that crossed the moon.

Seven score tattered hoods they doffed,
    They knelt on bended knee.
'Welcome, O welcome, master dear,
    Under the greenwood tree!'

Robin he stayed in the good greenwood
    For years full two-and-twenty.
He hunted, he robbed, but never again
    To Westminster palace went he.

Meanwhile in the musty cheerless court
    King Edward's hopes grew chill.
He waited, waited . . . And for all I know,
    He may be waiting still.